The First Five

Afterword Press

Artwork by: MasterPiece of MP Graphics

ISBN: 978-1-952555-08-4

The First 5

POEMS, STORIES, & PHOTOS
OF THE FIRST 5 YEARS WITH MY SON LANGSTON

Written by

Shawn William

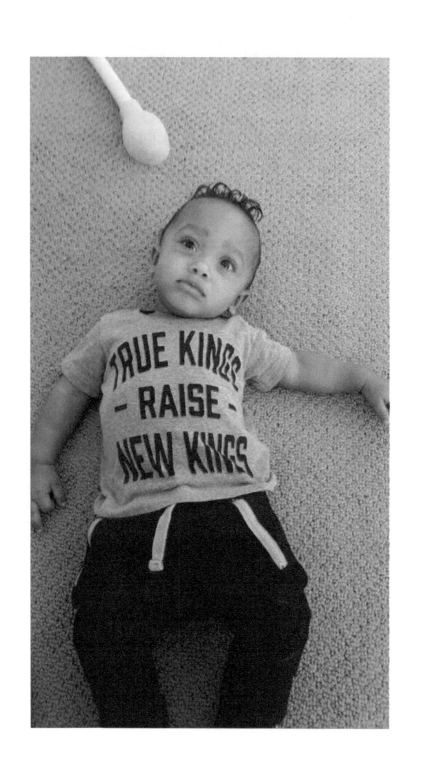

Introduction

"I love my child."

Said by millions of Black Fathers. So, what makes mine different? What makes my book any different from the millions of fathers out there?

One word: "Identity." Seeing my son helps me finally see me. This book is the journey of loving not only my son but also loving myself. It deals with a marriage and divorce. From being a stepfather to someone's son to someone trying to step in to be a stepfather to my son. It's dealing with depression, being on the spectrum, financial issues, career changes, & dating.

This book is a four part series written from the eyes of a father who is private with his son, letting the world see what their love looks like.

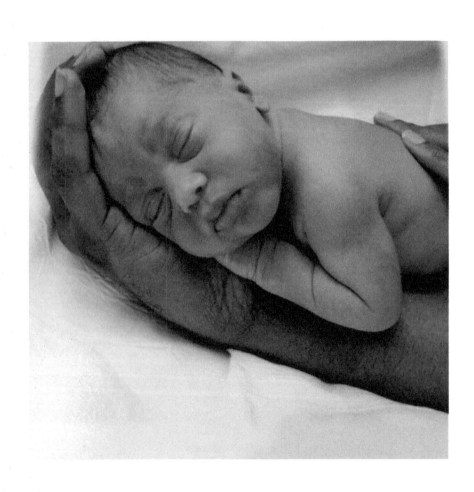

Acknowledgments

First and foremost, I'd like to thank My Lord and Savior for providing me so many blessings. "There would not be no me without you."

Thank you to my ex-wife & mother of my two children, Dontea. Though we do not always see eye to eye, we keep our eyes on the prize which is to co-parent this amazing child of ours to the best of our abilities. I thank you for your sacrifices and hard work.

Thanks to Langston's grandparents, aunt, cousins, and extended friends and family. Thanks to my best friend Antoni (Tone) Malloy and friend Janae. Your words and support during tough times were invaluable. Thank you to Kelly Freeman-Ceballos. I miss you so much. Our countless conversations while you were battling cancer helped fuel this book.

Thanks goes out to all my supporters and followers. The countless people who donated to help fund this journey. Thanks to the Afterword Press team for the relationship we've built. Thanks to My Brother's Keeper, the spoken word community, the promoters, radio DJ's, podcasters, & bloggers.
dri
Thanks to all the fathers that I reach out to for strength and guidance because just because I'm an Aries, doesn't mean that I think I know everything. Thanks to all the mothers who have given me tips. To Dads Evoking Change, Dear Fathers, and other social media outlets for allowing me to display my work on your platforms. To my father Tom, who taught me what a man really looks like and what to do and not to do. To my Uncle Wayne and Uncle Charles "Man", for being great mentors and role models in my life. To my Stepson Trey, initially my job was to play an important role in your life while teaching you, but I feel that you taught me a lot of lessons too. I wish the outcome was different. I will always love you no matter the circumstances.

Lastly to my Son Langston, this book is a reminder of my love for you. It is to let you know that when I leave this earth you will never wonder if I love you. That all those pictures and videos, some when you weren't in the mood, were taken for a reason. That this book and other things put in place are securing your financial future. I can never repay you for all the joy you've given me, but I can at least try to put it into words how I feel.

Table of Contents

Year 1

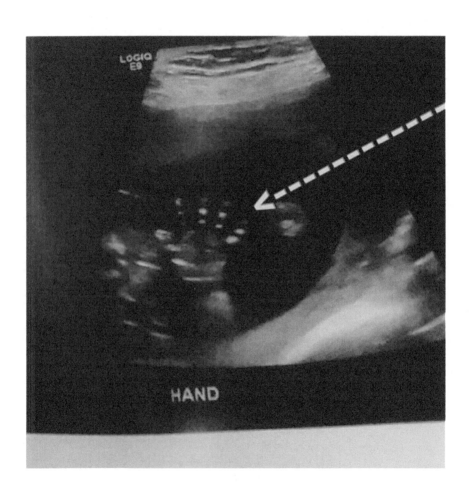

I Almost Caught a Case

Dear Son,

There's a chance that I won't be around when you're born
So I want to apologize now just in case I'm in jail
It's not what you're thinking
Let me explain
When your mother's water broke
I took her to the hospital and was met by a nurse
That asked her, "Are you sure your water broke? It might be pee."
If your mother wasn't having contractions she might have slapped the shit out of her
After finally getting into our room
We came across more rude staff members
That didn't sterilize
Forgot to wear gloves
Making jokes
Taking their sweet ass time
Everything moves so fast when you see red
But I think I said something to the extent of
"Are you going to move your ass or do I have to?"
That's what type of Father you have Son,
A man that will move mountains or lazy ass medical staff workers
To make sure the world is a better place for you.

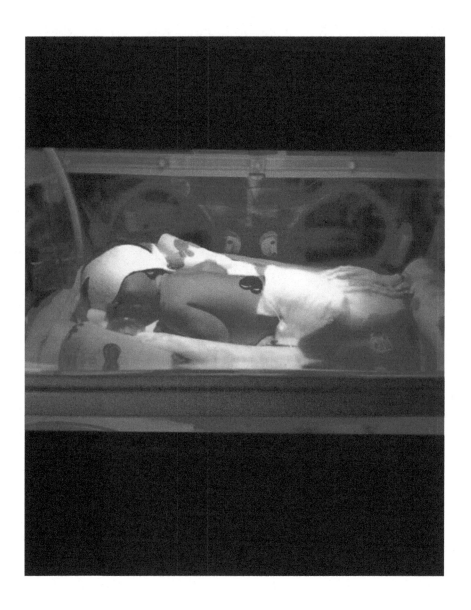

N.I.C.U. Glass

When you've waited decades to see your reflection
Physically and emotionally felt love for the very first time
Prayed for mother & child's weakened heartbeats to keep beating
Midwife screaming at your wife to give life because every second
passed risks his life
Dodging C-section and breaches
Cut eyes at slow moving medical staff
To finally cutting the umbilical cord

"YOU DID IT!"

The last thing that you want to hear is "We have to take him to
N.I.C.U."

For 6 days, I couldn't touch my son
I was only able to stare at him from behind glass
It was like some reverse prison scene from a 90's flick
Between father & son directed by John Singleton
But I was the one waiting for his release date. Every. Single. Day.

The worst part was that he couldn't see me.
So I sang to him, hoping that he could hear
Jill Scott, MJ, Stevie, Donnie, Jodeci
Anything so he could remember my voice

I hate hospitals
So every night I went home and slept by his crib on the floor
His mother stayed at the hospital, sleeping in an old recliner refusing
to leave his side

Home wasn't home if you weren't there Son
On the 7th day we took you home, kept you for 3 days, just to bring
you back

I cried so ugly

That was the day that I realized that I was human
That life was important
I didn't want to hear "It'll be ok"
Or

"My son went through the same thing"
All I wanted to do was hold my son
He needed me
I needed him
Doctors too busy
Staff didn't have answers
I'm a father who couldn't provide protection
Which made me feel useless
I just kept singing

Have you ever left N.I.C.U.
To get food for your tired wife
Come back to see the medical staff
Run past you with defibrillator in the direction of your child's room
While yelling "WE'VE GOT TO MOVE FAST HIS HEART STOP BEATING!"

Your heart will stop beating
You'll stand still but move closer
Like a Spike Lee movie trick
Just to find out that it's not your child's room they went into
So you thank God that it's not your child
It's another family
What a twisted and selfish thing to do

By now you know how the story ends
My Son was finally able to come home
Growing up healthy
So every time you see us together
We're touching, hugging, holding
We are whole

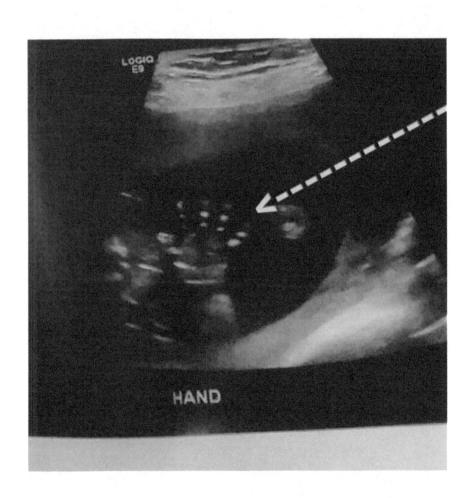

Hey Son Pt. 1

Hey Son, it's Daddy.
We finally came up with a name for you, it's "Langston."
Your Mother wanted "Harper," but that wasn't strong enough
And you are definitely strong
Like your mother
You weren't supposed to be here
Doctors told us that it would be a miracle if you came to fruition
But they're not God
God is God
And God said you were coming
Cancer couldn't stop a Cancer
See you soon

Marshawn & Langston

Cal Bear & Cal Boy

Marshawn & Langston chillin'

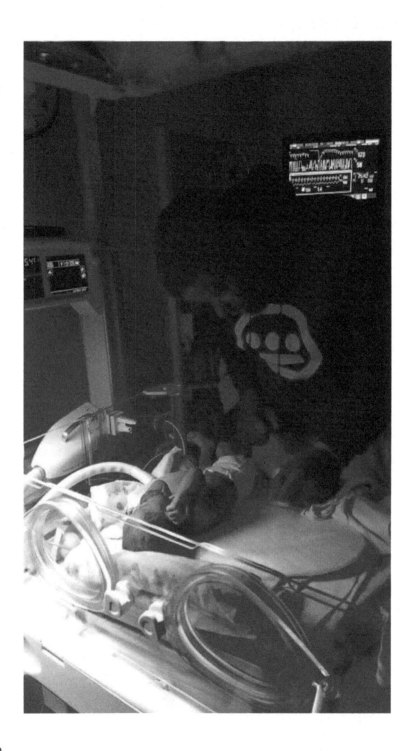

Hey Son Pt. 2

Hey Son,

Welcome to Oakland
I'm so glad that you're here
Tomorrow you'll be tested
To make sure that you can see and hear
Your mother's doing fine
She's over in the bed resting
Your Grammy's calling your Grampy
Grampy's calling your Uncles and Aunties
You have hella cousins
And a bunch of friends who are waiting to see you
But right now, it's me and you Son
This is our time
Our time

Adore

"Until the end of time
I'll be there for you
You are my heart and mind
I truly adore you
If God one day struck me blind
Your beauty I'll still see
Love is too weak to define
Just what you mean to me" – Prince

Let There Be Light

Heavenly Father, please continue to shine your light on My Son
And let every needed door be opened for him to walk through

Say It With Me

Repeat after me

"My job is to protect, provide, love, and break generational cures"
"My job is to protect, provide, love, and break generational cures"
AGAIN
"My job is to protect, provide, love, and break generational cures"
SAY IT AGAIN
"My job is to protect, provide, love, and break generational cures"
AGAIN!
"My job is to protect, provide, love, and break generational cures"
AGAIN!
"My job is to protect, provide, love, and break generational cures"
AGAIN!

Fat Meat IS Greasy

Is this a sign that my son won't believe it until he feels it?

In My Shoes

The reason why I didn't name you after me is because
I'm still trying to figure out who I am so why would I put that burden on you?
You will not be "the 2nd" you will be "The First"
To know who your biological father is
To hear "I love you" from someone that looks like you
You will not "Fill my shoes"
You will walk your own path
Whatever High School memories I had are irrelevant
You might look like me, but you will not be like me
You will be better
Bolder
More confident
Able to be both valuable and vulnerable
Get hugs and kisses
As long as I'm alive you'll never not hear "I love you" from me
"Filling my shoes" is low hanging fruit
And our family tree starts biologically with you and me
"Peaches" definitely put in on it
So Grow

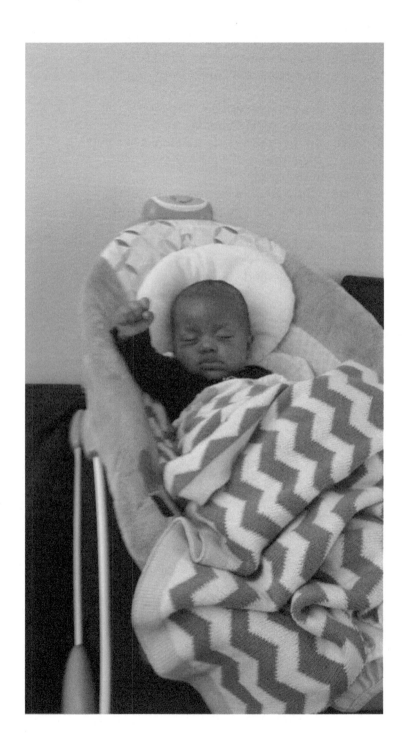

Dream

Dream Revolutionary My Son
Be eloquent as Dr. King
Stern like Malcolm
Gather troops like Hampton
But be intentional like T'Challa

No need to "Paint the White House Black"
But make sure that you're a black man that owns several
houses
And in that home teach your children that black is beautiful
And powerful

Your skin and features are the most feared and emulated
Dissected & hated
Focus on You more than "They"
Because "They"
Will tell You that "it wasn't that bad"
That you are respected more as entertainment than as an equal
They will let their sons listen to your music
But won't allow their daughters to listen to your love
So love You more
And worry about "Them" while worrying about "Them Less"

You are from Oakland so Panther and Warriors flow through
your veins
Always remember that
So put your right hand up
Close it and grab a dream
Never forget where you came from
And always know that you're a King.

Good Morning!

I'll do anything for that smile.

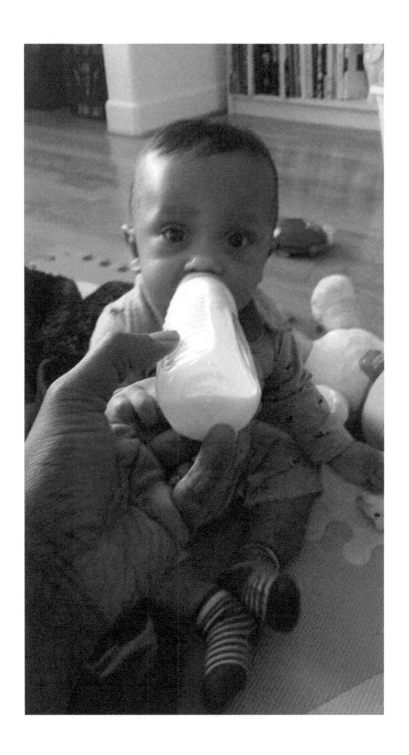

When Dads Take Over

"Where's Mommy?"

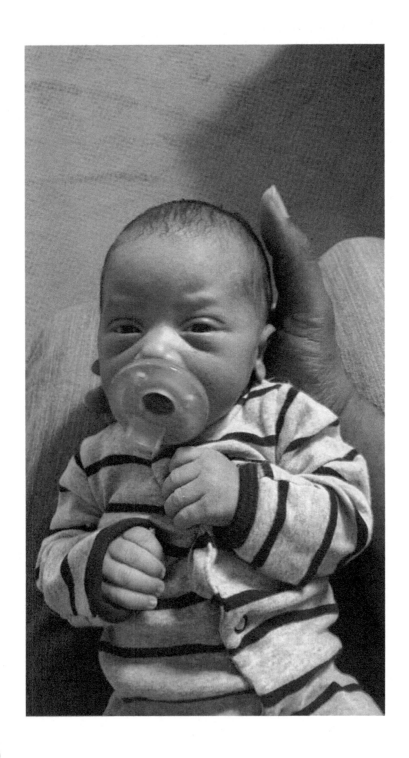

Hangry

Look Pops,
I'm hungry
And you don't look like you have what I need
So where's Mommy?
All that singing and cooing is cute and all
But if I don't get something in my stomach
I'm going to keep you up all night like I did
The last 2 nights
Oh, and you need to check my diaper

GO TO SLEEP!!!!

Please?
Pretty Please?
Just for 30 minutes?
20?
5?

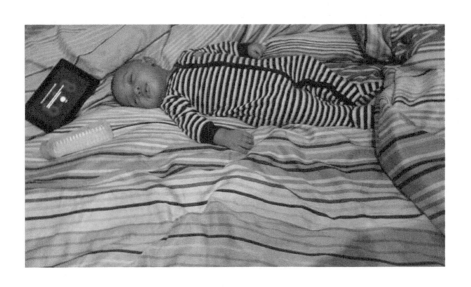

A Parent's Prayer

Father God, we thank you for the strength to get this child to sleep
We also thank you for creating the person that created the "White Noise" sound app
Thank you for breast milk, formula & patience.

Amen

Dad's Nice on These Sticks

I beat him 87-0
I don't care how young he is,
If you touch the controller that means you want smoke.

CPS

So today's the first day I'm home with My Son alone
And his mother's first day back to work.
She called me 5 times asking "Is the baby ok?"
My mother called me 3 times asking "Is My Grandson Ok?"
Her mother called me 2 times asking "Is My Grandson Ok?"
My sister called me asking "Is My Nephew Ok?"
Nobody called to ask me if "I'm Ok?"
And why are they calling so much anyway?
All I'm doing is taking pictures of My Son
Sitting in his car seat next to a bottle of Moet......

Extra Pt. 1

All I did was turn off Baby Shark

Passed Down

You will not be my "Lil Pimp"
Or inherit my misogyny
You can play an instrument or sports
But will not be taught how to play women

I will not have strippers waiting to
Initiate you into what immature men think is masculinity
That's both Boosie and "Bootsy"

We will talk about consent
Rape culture
That wearing down a woman to say "Yes"
Is not "Game" it's "coercion"

You don't have to ask women for pictures
Because if they like and respect you enough
Trust me, they'll send them to you

Open doors
Pull out chairs
Walk on the outside
Learn from broken hearts
But don't let them shape you

There will be boys who don't have loving fathers
Who will call you a "Simp"
And women who don't have fathers will call you "Square"
While putting you in the "Friend Zone"
But stand on your square son
Not everyone is worthy of a future King

And trust me, you are just that. A Future King.

Bedtime Stories and Stuff

"If I die before I wake?" That's morbid

"Good night, don't let the bedbugs bite" - Why do you allow your child to sleep in bedbugs?

"God is great, God is good, let us thank You for our food" - God deserves better bars than that

A Poem

This is a poem
In the flesh
Breathing
Living
Smiling
Co-written by two love birds
And edited by God

Biggie Smalls

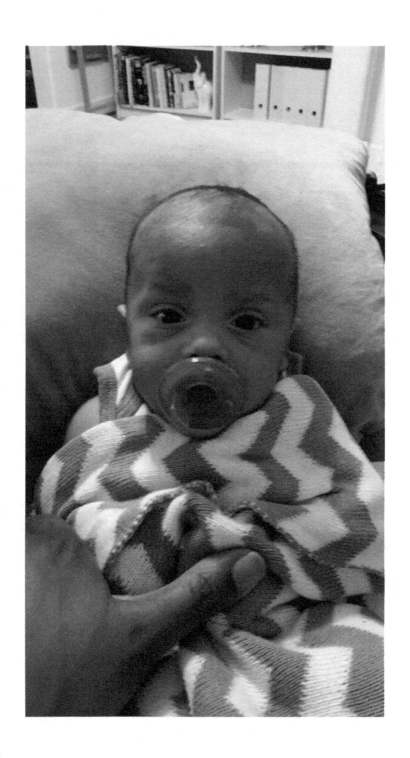

The Doctor Said.....

The Doctor said that your skull won't be fully formed until you're
4 or 5 years old
And that made me very sad.
The timeline is normal
But I've been waiting to body slam you like we're professional
wrestlers for a while.
I would be Sting
You Hulk Hogan
The ed would be our ring
You above my shoulders screaming "Daddy wait"
Me giving you the DDT or Piledriver
But I can't
Because we don't want you to have "brain damage" *rolls eyes*

I Wish I Was a Little Bit Taller

Don't even trip
The doctor said that you're in the 98 percentile
Which means that you'll be much taller than me
So prepare yourself to have people bring you out
Size 11 ½ shoes when you asked for 14's
Old ladies asking for help at the grocery store
And short dudes taking the business class seats on Southwest
Airlines

Paw-Paw

Did you know that your Paw-Paw was born in Texarkana?
That when he accidently cut off his finger on the table saw he picked it up,
Walked over to his helper, blood spilling,
And asked him to drive him to the hospital because he didn't think he could do it himself?
Did you know that your Paw-Paw build a house?
No, not the house you go to for holidays
He built the house I lived in back in the days. Oh, and built your Great Grandmother's 2nd house. He designed them too.
Did you know that your Paw-Paw was in magazines?
Yeah, because of his cabinet making.
That he's the smartest man I've ever met?
That his mind is so sharp that if the government
Would give him a chance, he could change the world for the better?
Did you know that he was my hero?

Top 5 NBA Players of All Time

Dear Son, here are the Top 5 NBA Players of All Time.

Magic
Kareem
Kobe
Shaq
Lebron

Honorable Mention to some dude named "Michael"

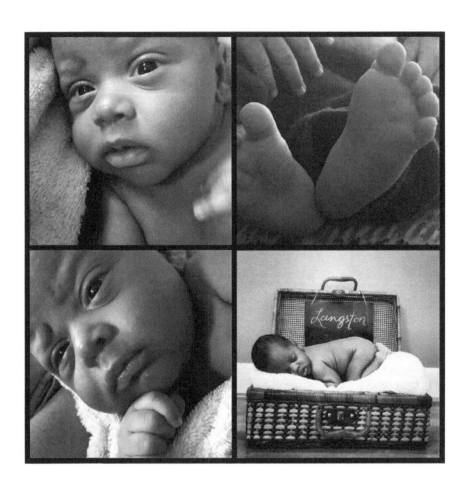

59

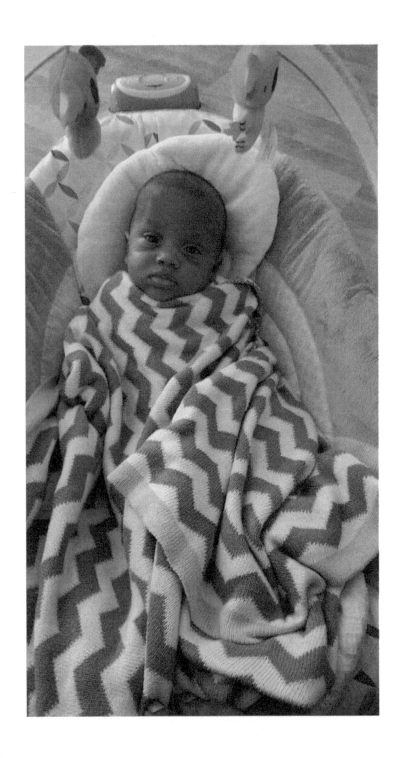

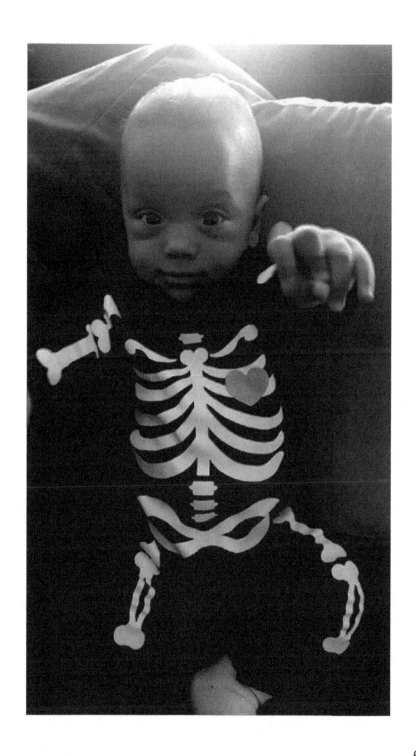

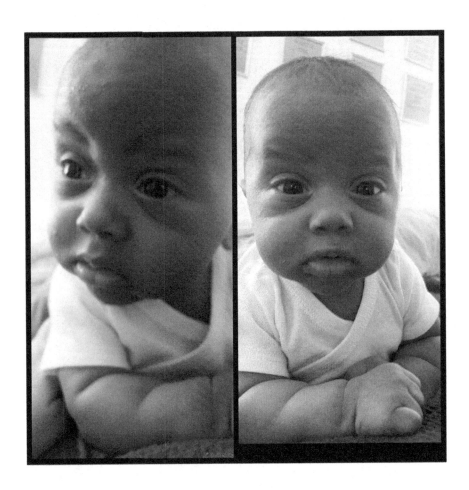

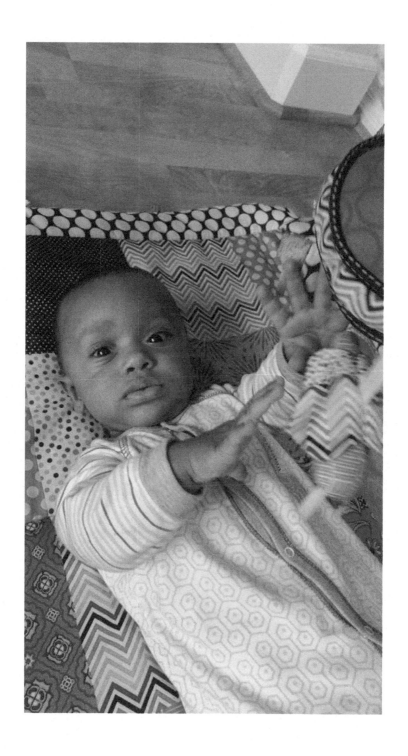

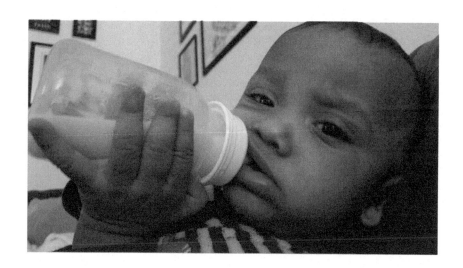

Year 2

Filled Shoes

Don't try to fill my shoes
Walk your own path
I didn't name you after me
Because I'm still trying
To find out who I am through you

I will not push you towards basketball, poetry, or misogyny
Things that I once or still do excel at
I will allow you to be great at whatever inspires and pushes your
passion
I will be more cheerleader than critic or sideline reporter
A "Fanboy" of my boy
There for you when you fall
And rise
And fall again

This is life
But it's your life
So live it for you

74

Get the Job Done

2:37am on a Tuesday
You had a fever
And I had a job interview
We stayed up until 104.1° went down to 98.3°
Ice cubes
Wet washcloth
Prayer & walks
It was only for 3 hours and 21 minutes
Just enough time for us to get a blink of sleep

For those who are wondering the outcome
I didn't get the job, but I got the job done

That's Daddy!

Weird huh?
Daddy's on TV
I'm not as famous as Peppa Pig
Or Paw Patrol
But I've toured the world
And made a few dollars

Breaking Generational Curses

"My parents beat my ass & look how I turned out."

Divorced
Womanizing
Unable to be emotionally available
To anyone that tries to get close & love you unconditionally
You lack humility
Seem narcissistic with pent-up anger issues
Yeah, you're financially stable, graduated college
& own multiple properties
But you have problems showing affection unless it's when
having sex
And never take accountability

Question: If your wife said or didn't something out of line
Would you physically discipline them?
How about a coworker, someone in management, or in law
enforcement?

Of course you wouldn't because self-control is used for adults
But control is the adult whose child has no say, or place to go

"I do it because the streets are much tougher"
That's a lie

"Putting children on Timeouts is white people shit"

Not realizing that beating black bodies in the name of love and
bible scriptures so they'll obey
Is the whitest thing you could ever do

Look, I'm not a saint
Or going to lie to you say that I've never popped my child
But after seeing the data out there and his face after
Knowing that I am one of the first people they will love
Knowing that his mind isn't fully developed
And there's no way he could ever understand how

His "Protector" is causing pain
And afterwards we're supposed to eat ice cream
And watch TV together
While saying something a slave master would say
"I only do this because I love you"

Really?

The Face They Give

The face they give you when…

- They want a cookie
- They want to stay up a little bit longer
- You tell them "Daddy has to go"
- You tell them "No, you can't have a giraffe"

I took my son to the doctor's to get his shots for the first time. I sat my son in my lap as the doctor put the needle in his tiny little arm. My son looked at me with this face and then tears streamed down his face. It felt like he thought that I betrayed him. That I allowed this monster to stick him in the arm and cause pain. I wanted to beat the hell out of that doctor. Stomp him out like Caine and O-Dog did Lina's cousin in the movie "Menace to Society" for making my son cry.

So after, I got him cookies, didn't leave until he went to sleep, and priced giraffes on Amazon.

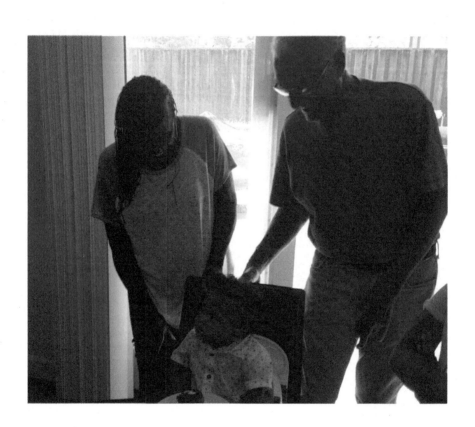

Transparent Grandparents

Son,

You call them "Grammy" & "Grampy"
But I'm here to tell you they aren't who you think they are.
As a matter of fact, I don't know those "Ninjas"
They are either the Aliens or Feds disguised as your
grandparents
Because when they were MY parents
Oh, man. They were wild.
They didn't coo and "awwww"
They scolded and said things like "Oh, hell naw!"
They believed in belts and switches
I once witnessed you walk over to "Grammy's" living room
With chocolate all over your hands
And proceeded to wipe your dirty fingers on her white couch
"Grammy" walked towards you,
I started writing your obituary in my head with tears in my eyes
Because I knew that I was about to lose you.
She opened her mouth and said "Look at what this cute little
baby did."
She picked you up and kissed you.
That was it
That's all she did.
No, I lied. She also gave you a snack

I said "What the f**k just happened?"
Because the woman that I knew growing up
Would've cursed me out like a drunken sailor during fleet week
While whipping me like cake batter

I don't know who these people are son
But they sure aren't "Grammy" & "Grampy"
And if they are them
Under all that grey hair
And fake smiles
They are two old people trying to get into heaven
For all the hell they caused me, when I was growing up.

Adopt-Shawn

When the doctor asked, "Does your family have a history of cancer, diabetes, or high cholesterol?"

I replied, "I don't know Doc, your guess is as good as mine."

And that was the day that I started looking for my biological family because this burden shouldn't be left on My Son.

Hugs & Kisses

Kiss your Sons fellas
When they upset you
When they make you happy
When they succeed
When they fail
Whenever

They shouldn't just be for your daughters
It's not "Gay"
"No Homo"
It's helpful
It's needed

And while you're at it
Hug your Sons Fellas
When they upset you
When they make you………

They Say...

They say that "Readers are leaders"
Well lead on, Young Prince. Lead on.

Little A** Blessings

Children are blessings
Gifts
Wise
Wonderful
But they're also assholes
They lie like shit
And only tell the truth at the wrong times
Example:
Langston – "Daddy, why does that big lady with the hairy lip keep looking at us?"
Or
Langston – "You're breathing heavy, maybe you should work out more"

Assholes

They will break your self-esteem and self-confidence if you let them

"You're wearing THAT to your show?" – Langston the Asshole
"Mommy got another new car" – Langston the Asshole
"This doesn't taste like spaghetti" – Langston the Asshole

They will walk all over you if you let them.
Parents don't let them

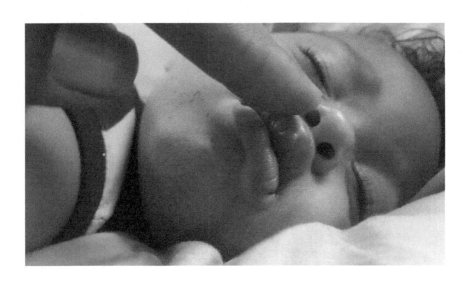

Petty

Remember that time you woke me up at 1:37am?
Then again at 4:37am?
And that time at 3:13am the next day?
And like clockwork the week before at 2:17am?
Well, payback is a mutha f…………

The First Haircut

Today was a monumental day for my Son,

The first haircut. A Father & Son bonding moment. Even though his mother and I are no longer married, I made sure that this was MY moment with him and in returned I had to "save a little for his book. A curl or two" for her.

For 6 months, I've prepared my son for this day. We held clippers and liners so he could get used to the clicking sound and vibration. I didn't know if he would be a screaming child, if I needed to have him sit on my lap or he'd just jump out the chair running for freedom.

He's 2 ½ years old with a headful of hair ready to be chopped. There were two barbers that I wanted to have the honors: Richard Gumbs, my ole barber, who moved off to Hollywood to produce movies, music, and occasionally cut the hair of A-list celebrities, and my other barber Maurice who once cut my stepson's hair, but he too went off to bigger and better things. So my only other option was this place called "Mark's Barbershop," a known spot in the bay area.

Langston was fine until I put him in the chair, a tear streamed down his face. A young boy asked him "Why are you crying?" and gave him one of his toys which made Langston feel cool.

The barber consoled him, patrons did as well as I said "You're doing fine son" while feeding him pieces of fruit rollups like my father once did me on my first haircut.

This was "Back Excellence" Male bonding. Black men who I've never met patting me on the shoulder & giving me support and praise. When it was all over, the barbers gave my son a standing ovation. My son felt special. The cashier handed him a sucker and he lit up like a Christmas Tree. I then had him give all the barbers and the little boy who gave him the toy first bumps.

To quote O'Shea Jackson "Today was a good day"

I love this little dude and my community

My Son's "Ugly" Face Saved You

When they told me (on Facebook) that my child was "ugly"
I sent a text to my friend that knows how to pull an IP address
Looked up flight prices
And wondered how I could stomp a mudhole in someone's ass
And then get ghost
But before I could click "Send" or "Purchase" I looked
At this picture of my Son and said to myself "Sheeeeit, they're tripping. My Son is the shit"

My Son saved your punk ass

Beautiful Parents

You are looking at a man: That has dealt with war most of his life
Langston is my peace.
Shallow men brag about making "beautiful children"
But my son makes beautiful parents.

How the Beef Started

When My Oakland Raiders played Her Atlanta Falcons
A bet was made

I lost the bet so My Son ended up wearing this all day.

She played songs by Luda, T.I., & Jeezy all day.
I put him in a Raiders jersey hella times and he NEVER looked this
damn happy.
This some bull***

Breakfast in Castro Valley, CA.

This picture was taken at an eatery in Castro Valley, CA.
A white woman came up to our table and
Complimented how handsome my son was
She seemed fascinated by his "Curly hair"
And looked at me like a unicorn
As if she's never seen black men with their children
I waited like it was the 95 AC transit bus
Taking me to my old house on Pickford
For her question
"What is he mixed with?"

It was as if another race was needed
To make this child beautiful
Instead of just two in love at the time people
Creating this handsome child

I pray that people like this woman all die off
By the time my child is able to take his child out to breakfast
And that he doesn't inherit my anger towards ignorant people

Because he deserves much better
All our children do

Poo-Tang Clan

Child Rules Everything Around Me C.R.E.A.M. he gets all My money. Dollar, Dollar Bill Y'all.

The 1000 Words this Photo Said

This photo is beautiful huh?
Peaceful
Happy
But would you be surprised if I told you
That for the last 4 days I was living at my job?
No, not "living" like working hard for hours
I mean "living" at my job, sleeping there because
I was without a home.
I left a million dollar home by the water
To live in a break room, sleeping in a massage chair
Locking the door from the inside hoping security didn't come in
When they checked the building
Then, I wake up around 4:30am before the first shift came in
Go wash myself in the bathroom
Come in to work extra hours (Because I needed the money)
And do it again for 4 more days until my room was ready
In Deep East Oakland.
No, not "apartment" "room"
I didn't have the money to put 3 grand down
For an apartment
So I rented a room

And this picture
This picture was taken at a Starbucks in El Cerrito
It was first time I saw Langston in over a week
Because I didn't have any place to keep him.
We were sitting and waiting for a former co-worker
Who I was borrowing money from
I just needed a couple of hundred dollars
To pay off pass due bills because all I had left that was strong
Was my credit.
My will to live or even survive was a distant 2nd
I wanted to off myself several times but didn't
Because of this face
This face was what made me figure it out
This face was what made me want to get stronger
This face was my face
My sunshine that I needed because all I saw was rain
This face touched my face and said "Hi Daddy"
And I didn't want to leave this Earth never hearing that again.

Thank You Son. You don't know it, but this was the day
That you saved Daddy's life.

Year 3

True Kings Raise New Kings

"True Kings Raise New Kings"
To love
To live
To love living
Living Free
Loving Free
Freedom is a quest that I don't want you to take a lifetime to find
Freedom is peace
Freedom is peace of mind
Your spirit will guide you there
Your heart will keep you there
Love is your Kingdom My Prince
Rule correctly My Prince
Unselfishly
Unapologetically
Unconditionally
With a Queen by your side
That has your back
And will never front
Rule My Prince
Rule

Stage Presence

My son has been on stage with me since the age of 2
He never cried
Never wanted to get off
Look at him
Staring at the mic like he's about to eat
Imagine what's going through his mind
Look at his eyes
His focus
My Son
I'm not grooming him to be a poet, singer, or rapper
I'm just training him to never fear speaking in front of people
Because his voice is too important to be silent

Invisible

Me- "Langston, what are you doing?"
Langston- "I'm invisible. You can't see me"
Me- "Huh?"
Langston- "I'm invisible, you can't see me"
Me- "Yes, I can. You're right there."
LANGSTON TAKES 3 STEPS FORWARD
Langston- "No I'm not."
Me- "OMG, YOU ARE INVISIBLE!"
Langston- "I told you"

Oakland Boy Pt. 1

"Just Win Baby"

Beautiful Banter

It took you a while to talk
It took you longer to complete a sentence
You were silent
"Nonverbal"
We didn't know when you'd start talking
Or ever speak at all
Fast forward and you talk about everything
Paw Patrol
Roblox
The Cat with one eye
Mommy's "New friend"
If I had a dollar every time you asked "Daddy look" I'd be on
Jay-Z status
You talk so much that sometimes I want to ask, "Langston can
you please be quiet?"
But then remember back I'd often asked, "Langston can you
please say something?"
And then I'd put whatever it was that I was doing down, look at
you and listen to that beautiful banter.

The Talk

I'm no longer with your mother
A decision that I feel was mutual
Reasons why can be fully explained
On your 18th birthday
Sipping a cold one
While watching an A's game
That is if they're still around
Speaking of "around," I will be
There's nowhere else I'd rather be
Than with my reflection
The agreement is that
I have you 3.5 days
She has you 3.5 days
We went "half on a baby"
And now we're going half on custody
Joint, straight to the point
We'd both be too weak
If we let a week go by.
I will not be a "Weekend Dad"
All promises of raising you
Loving and being there for you
Whenever you need me
Will still be kept
We just won't all be in the same home
You'll have two of everything
But the mission is still the same one
Loving you correctly
Unconditionally
Forever

3.5

3.5 Days
50/50 Joint Custody

That is what we agreed on
And that's what's happening
Neither your mother nor I could go a week without you
And I damn sure wasn't going to be a "Weekend Father"

I enjoy dropping you off and picking you up from school
And having our Sunday breakfast

Judah, The Slap and a Bag of Weed

My son Langston smacked the shit out of a little kid at school today.
Too soon? My bad, let me tell the entire story.
I took Langston to school today.
He like his Father isn't a morning person
He'll get up, but he's not all "Warm and fuzzy"
So when we walk into his class 6 kids yelled out "LANGSTON!!!!!"
They then ran up to My Son and gave him a group hug
Langston wasn't feeling it.
His teacher, Mrs. Pen said to the hugging children
"Now kids, what did you teach you about personal space? Do not hug anyone unless they are ok with you hugging them"
Something I thought was cool, because back in my day, if somebody wanted to hug you, then. You got hugged. Even if they were musty.
So 5 of the 6 kids stopped hugging Langston, except Judah.
Judah, kept hugging Langston
So Langston nudged him off of him with his elbow
I watched
Judah then hugged Langston again
I watched
Langston pushed Judah off him
I watched
Judah, then punched Langston in the stomach
I watched, then was about to react
But before I did, Langston open handed smacked the shit out of Judah.
Judah fell down to the ground
BAM!
I said "Damn"
Judah's mother (Who was also there) yelled "Oh My God"
Judah's mother ran over to her Son
Picked him up and asked "Did you see what your son did?"
With I smile I said "Yup, Sure did"
Judah's mother then asked "Do you think that was ok?"
I replied "I sure do"
She then said "I don't know what teach your child in your home, but in MY home, violence is never the answer and children should keep their hands to themselves"
Where I replied "Well in MY home, I teach Langston if anyone puts their hands on him he has my permission to smack them and since

Judah is a demon that doesn't know how to keep his hands to himself...welp"

She was appalled and I was a proud parent.

I felt so good that when I went to get my haircut later that day I walked into the barbershop and said "Hey fellas, My Son Langston smacked the shit out of this kid at school today!"

I got a free haircut.

One dude gave me a bag of weed

My credit score went up 86 points

I reenacted to slap several times, from different angles, slow motion too.

I'm upset that the slap wasn't recorded

My Son comes from a long line of slappers who teach demons how to keep their hands to themselves.

Violence may not "be the answer" like Judah's mama thinks but it show eliminates a lot of questions.

Oakland Boy Pt. 2

Langston will never say "International Blvd"
He will only go to Chipotle if the Taco Truck is gone
He will learn about Huey P, Felix Mitchell, The Red Fence,
Dorsey's Locker & East Bay Dragon's Parties
He will know that Oakland influences the world
I will teach him about Oscar Grant & Lovell Mixon
Frank Somerville < Dennis Richmond
When he's 14, I will purchase a primer Mustang 5.0 for us to
work on, get painted, Pony Rims with 'Slap' in the back, for us to
one day drive on Sundays and then later give to him on his
18th Birthday.
I will randomly ask him Oakland questions: "The Year Ricky
Henderson broke the stolen base record?"
"Besides being a gun, what else is 357?" & "What's the fast way
to the Oakland Airport?"
Around me, "Hella" isn't a "bad word", it's a way of life.

Oakland Boy

Big Boy Pants

Fellas,
Make peace with your child's mother.
Forgive your child's mother.
Have a solid relationship with your child's mother.
Send flowers on Mother's Day to your child's mother.
Provide presents on her birthday.
It might not be a nuclear family
But you sure don't want to cause a nuclear war
I know, I know
But your Daughter needs to see a man love her even
Though he's no longer in love with her
Your Son needs to see how to respect a woman
Even if you do not like that woman
Because "that woman" gave birth to them
And they love her unconditionally
So put on your "Big boy pants"
And put down your pride
Be the bigger man
For them
For you
For peace

Know the Game Son

Play the world, don't let the world play you.

One Thing's for Certain, 2 Things for Sure

My Child will learn about Hip Hop

The Rankings

Langston came home from school with an assignment that asked "Name 3 things that you love"

He listed them in this order:

1. Mommy
2. Cheez-it
3. Daddy

I have no problem with my Son loving His Mother more than me, but Cheez-it? I come 3rd to some damn snack? I mean they're good and all but come on.

First Day at Pre-K

First day of Pre-K,
His Mother and I both nervous.
We've heard the stories
Little boys and girls having adjustment problems
Yelling, screaming, kicking, pleading not to be left alone.
But the only people that were crying
Were the parents.
He was good.

148

I Got Played by Pre-K Kid

I take Langston to Pre-K
When we get to his classroom we do the normal routine
Me: "You ready for school?"
Langston: "Yes"
Me: "Be strong, be brave, be beautiful"
Langston: "Ok"
Me: "I'm a King"
Langston: "I'm a King"
Me: "I am strong"
Langston: "I am strong"
Me: "I love myself"
Langston: "I love myself"

I give him a high 5 and send him on his way.
When I turnaround I see this beautiful chocolate little girl was looking at me with the biggest eyes. So not leaving her out I put my hand up to give her a high 5 as well. The beautiful chocolate little girl slaps my hand and smiles. We smile together sharing that moment. I turn back around to look at My Son and MY SON is looking at me like I betrayed him. Like I brought his once full tank car back with ¼ of a tank. If Langston could've said "I ain't f**king with you Dad" in that moment he would've. That day he probably drew a stick figure of me then crossed it out.
I tried to explain my case and he just walked off as the girl stood there smiling.

Damn, that little girl played me. She divided the Fam'.

Executive Decisions

A picture sent to me from Daycare:

My Son's been here before
Why is he standing in front of the snack pantry looking like he's about to make an executive decision?
Look at his hands behind his back
Shoulders straight
Head up
Why is the dog looking at him like "You're going to get in trouble, but if you don't can you share?"
Did Langston throw that snack on the ground?

I have questions

Malcolm X-Mas

What I won't do, is let some fictitious, old, drunk white man who has a sweatshop
Filled with little people get the credit for all the hard work I've done.
"Son we don't have a chimney. I drank the milk and ate the cookies.
I worked those 12 hours of OT, wrapped those gifts
Elbowed those people for that last bike
And drove to 3 stores to get that Nintendo Switch.
Ok, well that was ya Mama
But so, what.

"And by the way, Jesus was born in the Spring & reindeers don't fly."

The Power of a Child's Love

I hear parents say it all the time, but it still amazes me how in tuned a child is with their parents. Just a few minutes ago Langston gave me the biggest hug & "I love you" and it was right on time. Children see the bigger picture better than us complicated thinking grown people.

The homie Myishea said yesterday in a post "Langston makes you cooler." You don't even know the half.

Drink water
Love Yourself
Value your friendships
& trust ya kids.

Do Daddy

Me- "Langston, imitate Daddy"
Langston- "Go lay down, you're on time out!"
Me- *Laughs*

Maturity From a Once Violent Man

Do you know how many lives my son has saved?
How many times I wanted to put hands on dudes
Who talked reckless to me knowing that I could
Put blood in their mouths with a perfectly placed combo set up?

I've had violent visions of pistol whipping, backhand slapping
And stomping out a mutha f***a or two
But didn't because my responsibilities are first and foremost to
my son.

A lot of you are fortunate.
My son has matured me
Giving up my freedom isn't a thought anymore
I go home
Walk away without feeling the burn to get back
I now show my diplomacy because 3.5 days is long enough
Being away from my child
But 3-5 years is unheard of.

You're welcome

Giving Me My Flowers

The other day Langston and I were at the park
We walk by a patch full of baby daisies
When he decided to pick a few
I asked him "Are those for Mommy"
He looked my direction, presented them to me and said, "Daddies need flowers too."

This kid.

Daddy Issues

I have no problem with you dating again
I have no problem with you finding love with another man
I have no problem with that man being around our son
Because "It takes a village" right?
The problem that I have is finding out about this man from our
son instead of you
No, scratch that
The problem that I have is that our son is calling that man
"Daddy"
When he already has one
No, scratch that
The problem that I have was the reasoning why our son, who
has a father, is calling that man "Daddy"
No, scratch that
The problem that I have is that our son is calling that man
"Daddy" and you didn't talk to me about it
No, scratch that
The problem that I have is that our son is calling that man
"Daddy" and I haven't met this man
No, scratch that
The problem that I have is that our son is calling another man
"Daddy", while also having this man around our son for over a
year without me knowing

This is where I'm supposed to talk tough as shit
Threatened to break dude in two "if he ever....."
Burn bridges that just got rebuilt
Plus call you every name possible but your own given
But all I have for you is "Stop it"
Please "Stop it"
I'm not intimidated by him
Our Son knows who his father is
I'm not trying to get in the way of your love or your life
But that's not right
And deep down inside, you know that.

Update It stopped. Peacefully

Thinking Outside of the Box

For his 3rd birthday
I bought My Son
A black Mercedes Benz
G-Wagon 12-Volt Remote control truck
And you couldn't tell me SHIT that day

His mother, who has been winning the "War of Gifts"
The past two years
And today that streak was going to stop

So, when she dropped him off
His ride behind the door
He walks in and sees
The Black
Mercedes Benz
G-Wagon
12-Volt
Remote control truck
And yells "DAAAADDDYYY, I love you"
And isn't that the best gift a father could give his child?

As my son plays with his G-Wagon
I went into the kitchen to make dinner
All I could hear is "VROOOM", "ERRR" and other car noises
That was music to my ears
After 20 minutes I go into the room and see my son
Sitting in front of the TV
NOT in the black
Mercedes Benz
G-Wagon 12-Volt
Remote control truck
But in the box that it came in

I asked My Son "Langston, what are you doing?"
He replies "I'm at the drive-in movies waiting for food"

I tell him "Langston, get out of the box"
He whined "Noooooo"
 "Come on Langston stop"
He whined "Nooooooo"

"Langston, we're not doing this today"
I put him in the G-Wagon and that's when it happened

Transitions are difficult for children who are on the spectrum
Their screams come off like they're in excruciating pain
Like laying naked on shards of broken glass
Eyes searching for safety
Everything seems foreign including their parents
Looking like they're under attack
Physicians call them "Meltdowns"
As a parent you feel helpless
Self-conscious
Wondering if he had these meltdowns in public
What would people think of me and my son
Would they call me a "bad parent"?
Look at my son as a "Bad ass kid" that needs a beating
And taught a lesson?
And when my son gets older
Inheriting my height and hue
History has proven
That teachers, principals, and nosey 'Karens'
Will not be as kind and understanding as his mother and I
Confuse his fear with frustration and rage
Possibly call the police because this "bad ass kid needs a beating"
Be taught a lesson"
And that scares the living shit out of me
But right now, I can't think about the future
Just focus on the present
I no longer think about the present I gave him
Just think about the beautiful gift his mother gave me
So, after four of the longest minutes of my life
I ask my son for a hug
He, finally recognizes me, looking exhausted says "Yes"
We embrace as if we haven't seen each other in years
Both of our hearts beating fast
And THAT very moment I realize
That maybe it's not my son with the transition problems
Maybe it's us adults
That unlike his father,
My son loves living in the moment
He doesn't want his thoughts pigeon-holed
He thinks outside of the box

And a G-Wagon IS in fact the shape of….. a box
And that box can be whatever his wonderful imagination wants it to be
A spaceship
A castle
A speed boat
Or YES, even a Mercedes G-Wagon
So, I grab our meals and sit inside of the bo…. I mean "G-Wagon"
with my son
At the drive-in
As we eat dinner together on his birthday
Living and enjoying the moment
And isn't that the best gift, a father could give to his child?

The World Is Yours

Cuba
LA
Mexico
Puerto Rico
Hawaii
Disneyland
Legoland
Coming up Toronto, Disney World, Six Flags.......The World

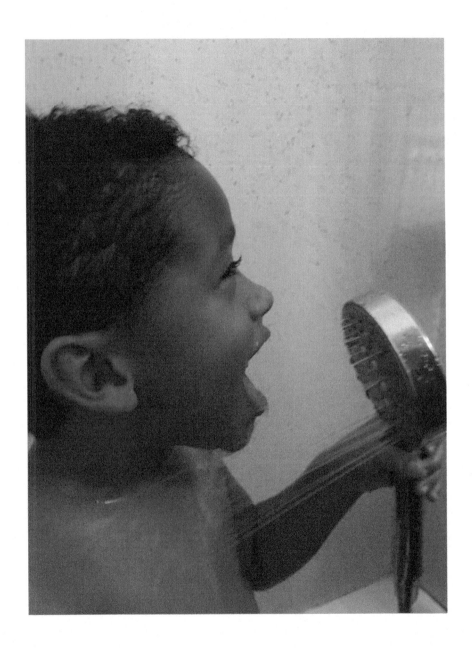

Langston's Ideas

"Daddy, they should make Microphones that shoot water. That would make your shows better"

Year 4

Looks and Look like Me

So this picture was taken of me
Looking at someone telling a story
And I knew that they were lying their ass off
Little did I know that Langston was side eying them too.

You can't tell me that he's not my son.

Wingman

Look, don't judge me
But Langston is the best wingman I've ever had
I try to use his power for cuteness for good not evil
But women love fathers who are single

The other day at Target, Langston said "I love you Daddy"
And this Baddie said "Awwwww"
Wait, it gets better
I replied, "I love you too son" and gave him a hug
Showing the Baddie that I'm a man
Who doesn't have a problem showing public affection
To my son while also being able to verbalize it

It was so cute Baddie asked me if I was open for a playdate

Langston is cute at Lake Merritt
Grocery Stores
The Gym
Starbucks
He's great
"Look, don't judge me"
I'm just spending quality time with my son
Wearing grey sweats
With my fresh cut
And beard oiled

The other day my friend offered me $50 if he could rent
Langston
For Juneteenth
He offered to feed him and everything
I had to decline
Because I was going to Juneteenth

Halloween

Until America gets its shit together
Langston will be Black Panther this year

"Wakanda Forever"

A Father's Warning Shot

This is a father's warning shot
A strong oath that if anything ever happens to my son
If you ever graze his beautiful face with Billy club or bullet
Confuse pistol for taser and label it "An accident"
I swear that "I will strike down upon thee with great vengeance and furious anger"
That you would've thought it was said by God or Samuel Jackson turning psycho

Something must change with these police officers that
Have hatred in their holsters
Using our children for target practice
But this poem is not to spark a "Change"
This is a father's warning shot
Letting you know as a father I've done
Everything in my power to make sure that my son will not be shot by you
So, I'm asking, for you to do everything in your power to not shot him
To "Serve and protect" him

You will not make me like Trayvon Martin's father because I am
Not that strong of a man
I know myself
I am weak and reckless
I do not have the time to sit in a courtroom
Listening to testimony testing my patience
From a prosecutor that normally sends black boys to prison
Hoping that this time he'll get it right
I do not have to see if they will get it right

You will not convince me that it took a "Radio Raheem"
Chokehold to take down my son
Forget that
I am his father
We play wrestle all the time

So, I know exactly how strong he is
His mother will not yell
"NO!"
Scream
"WHY?"
And if the day ever comes
That she comes to me with
Tears in her eyes
No breath in her lungs
Weakness in her legs
Asking me
Begging me
Yelling at me "SHAWN DO SOMETHING!"
As God as my witness
I will snap
Break
Scream
Kick
Forget a march
I will fly
Off the hinges
And "Release the Kraken"
Turning into the same "Beast" you thought my son was
When you pulled the trigger
Scratch that
I will turn into the same "beast" you were
When you pulled the trigger on my son
My son's name will not be used as a hashtag or a war cry
My son's face will not be put on T-shirts or on murals
My son will not have me and his mother dressed in all black
On the cover of a magazine holding a picture of him
My son is not a beast
My son is not a threat
My son will bury me
"I will not bury my son"
My Son
Langston
Lite enough to be a "Pretty Boy"
But dark enough to be considered a "Suspect"

182

And I know
Some of you may be asking
"Do you get this upset when it's a black-on-black crime?"
The answer is "No"
Because something just seems heinous and disgusting
Knowing that my hard earned tax dollars are being used
To pay hitmen to put hits out on my son

The only time a child should be taken away
From his parents is by the medical staff at birth
And when the staff checks the child & finds out they are ok
Their job is to give them back to their parents
So, when you see my son walking down the street
Or pulling him over for a "routine traffic stop"
I am asking
Begging you
To make sure he's able to come back home
This is not a poem
This is a Father's Warning Shot
Don Killuminati
Track 2
1st verse from Tupac
And I quote
"I aint a killa, but don't push me"

Black Boy Joy

Black Boy Joy in Cuba
Langston & Che

Talking to Daddy in Cuba

This picture was taken of Langston in Cuba
Talking to me on the phone
His smile while talking to me is everything

That's it
That's the poem

Represent!

"Daddy, he looks like Me!"

Representation is so important for little black children

Cheating A** Son of Mine

Langston- "Let's play superheroes"
Me- "Ok"
Langston- "I'll be Captain America"
Me- "Ok, I'll be Iron Man"
Langston- "Shoots web!"
Me- "Wait, Captain America doesn't shoot webs!"
Langston- "Turns invisible"
Me- "How?"
Langston- "Hulk Smash!"
Me- "Hulk? I thought you were Captain America?"
Langston- "I am"
Me- *walks away*

Boy Open The Door!

Me- "Open the door"
Langston- "Can we have McDonalds?"

Kids Hurt Your Self-Esteem

Langston & I *Watching videos on MY phone *

Text message pops up

Langston *Swipes right*

Me *Pauses video* "Hey, what are you doing?"

Langston- "It's not Mommy" *He presses "Play" and goes back to watching the video

God is Petty

They say that "Whatever you hate will be given back to you through your child" and Langston takes food off my plate when he has the EXACT same thing on his.

My Cancer Child

"Children should be seen and not heard" – Is this why so many children are afraid to speak to their parents about molestation?

"Spare the rod, spoil the child" – Did you know that slave owners said this to their slaves after beatings and many of our ancestors adopted that saying in their homes?

"I brought you into this world and I'll take you out of it" psychological warfare

And of course

"These kids nowadays are soft"

Look, I don't mind my child not being as hard as me. Being hard is overrated. Being hard is taxing emotionally. From 15 to 35, not once did I cry. Even if I was in pain or lost someone and now looking back I wish I did. I wish I was able to process pain better, but "being hard" wouldn't allow me to. You can't be hard and love correctly at the same time. "Hard" can break. Soft can't. I want my son to know how to defend himself physically, emotionally, and mentally and being "hard" won't all him to do all three.

So my Cancer son, whose sign is accused of being "so emotional," I sometimes think you cry so much because you're shedding the tears that I wasn't able to give.

Oh, He's BIG Mad?

Text from My Child's Mother
"Look at YOUR Son"

This picture is My One!
Arms crossed
Lip out
He's ready to go, go!
Look at him, a "Habitual Line Crosser"
If looks could kill, err'body be dead
This is what 'Hangry' looks like
He's mumbling curse words right now, I know it

What's Beef? Pt. 1

Two Proud Parents at Langston's Graduation:

Me- "Good job Mommy"
Mother- "Good Job Daddy"
GIVES DAPS
Me- "So you want his diploma?"
Mother- "No, you can have it."
Me- *SURPRISED* "Really, thanks"
Mother- "Yeah, I'm keeping his High School diploma and college degree"
Me- "Wow"

Year 5

Dear OUSD

Dear Oakland Unified School District,

I'm not your enemy,
A reflection of your ex,
Or a unicorn.
I am a black father who is a constant in my son's life
And I would like to be respected as such.
When I ask you, "How's my son doing?"
I would like the same answers that you give my child's mother.
Saying "He's doing fine,"
When he's not at times, is insulting.
I shouldn't be forwarded text messages from my child's mother
When my number is on file.
If there's a problem, please call me since I live
Three minutes away from the school.
It seems that teachers have a problem
Talking to black fathers because
They aren't used to seeing a lot of black fathers.
So whatever your assumptions are
Erase them.
Because you're going to see a lot of me
And if I don't get the answers I want
Just like my height
I will go over your head
Until my concerns about my son's education
His conduct
And his wellbeing
Are taken care of.

Sugar Baby aka What's Beef Pt. 2

His mother sent me this picture with a text saying,
"We're on our way, he wanted a donut first. Lol"
"Lol" hell. And NO, this picture is neither "adorable" nor "precious"
What you see is a cute picture of a boy eating a snack,
But what I see is a kid that's going to be on a sugar rush all night
Wanting to watch Moana for the 537th time when I just got into town
From doing a show in Seattle.

This some bullshit

Because.....

I asked my 5-year old son, "Why do you always want to lay on me?"
And he replied, "Because you're soft and cuddly."
I know this won't always be the norm, but today I'm glad it still is.

Extra Pt. 2

Why does My Son look like he's dreading to go work a 12 hour shift?
Like his first name is "James" and last name is "Evans Sr." and he's
"Keeping his head above water"?
Like there isn't any food in the refrigerator and he hasn't eaten in
days?
My Son really looks like he hasn't been to Disneyland, Cuba, Mexico,
Puerto Rico and Hawaii all before he turned 6.
Like he doesn't have 2 Nintendo Switches, a PlayStation & 4 living
Grandparents.
He looks like he's dealing with Reaganomics or the 90's Crime Bill
All this because he's going to a school that allows midday naps.
My Son is SO extra.

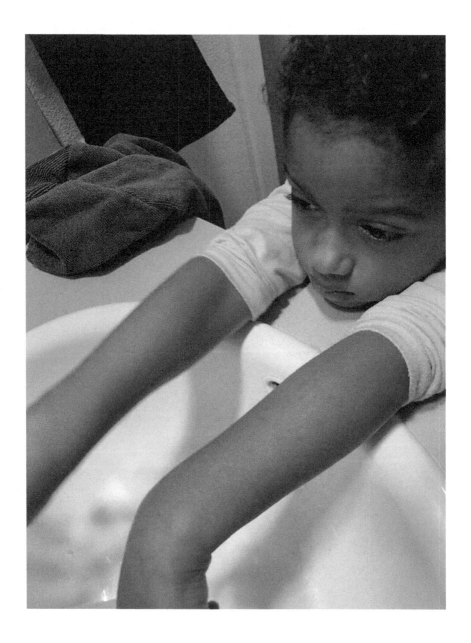

Top Boy

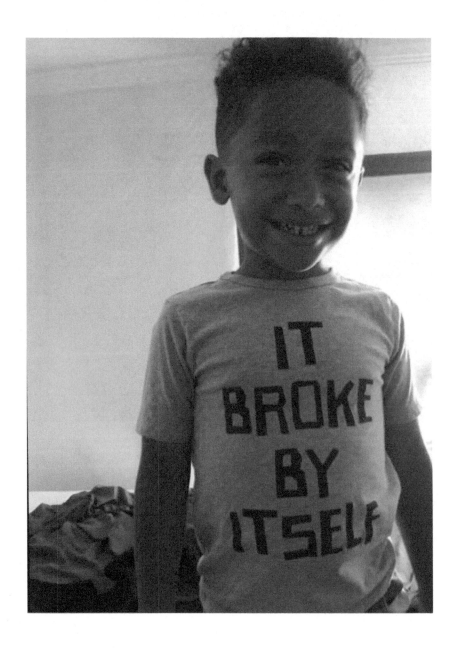

"Your Child"

Fellas, if you let them tell it, He's only "Your Son" when:

- They break something
- They lie
- They keep her up at night
- They get below a B average in school
- The teacher calls
- They lose something
- They have a blowout in their diaper
- They eat their boogers. And how do you know that you don't have any booger eaters in your family?
- He can't spell "Cat" after 10 tries and she's tired
- She needs a glass of wine or a Mexico trip

I'll leave space below fellas for you to add more. Stay Strong Kings.

5 Years at the Lake

Lord willing, we will do this every year
Or until the dead bodies in Lake Merritt rise & start chasing us down
Grand Ave.

Tradition

Well Groomed?

If I said the following to your 5-year-old daughter:
"She's going to be a heartbreaker"
"Look at her lips, I could just kiss them all day"
"I'm going to be her first boyfriend"
"Looking all fine like her mother"
"I could just play in her hair all day"
"She's filling into her body really well"
"All the boys are going to be chasing after her"
"You better watch out for this one, she's a cutie"

Would you be ok with it?

Then why do you say those things to my 5-year-old son?

Color this picture of a boy sitting on his dad's shoulders.

Thanks Black Joy Parade

When the Oakland City Libraries have you and your son in their coloring books………

Man!

Dating While Being a Dad

I date differently now that I have Langston
Every woman is judged from a new lease
I'm not looking for Langston's mother because he already has one
But I am looking at how you maneuver with children even your own
Do you have patience?
Are you reliable?
Do you ask about my son?
Do you send ideas of things for us to do?
Do you respect my time with him or are you selfish without understanding?
I've dated a lot of women since my son's been on earth
Only one was close to being worthy
She's beautiful, caring and has a kind spirit
I truly believe that my son would fall for her just like I did
But unfortunately we didn't work out
And the chance for a Queen to meet my Prince never came
And though I was sad
I was also fortunate
It was for the best
Because I don't want myself and my son to have to deal with the pain
Of losing a wonderful woman
I'll take that L for L

Boushy Son

Parenting During the Pandemic

One of the most depressing things about the pandemic
Was seeing children in masks
I know this is what they need to help stop the spread
And contracting the COVID-19 virus
But seeing your child on the playground
Or at the park playing
Having their breathing restricted
Just doesn't seem like they're getting the full childhood
experience

To this day My Son is afraid to remove his mask
I know that it's for his own safety
But I just don't like it.

The Impression You Make vs. the Impersonation You Receive

About the Author

Shawn William is an award winning spoken word artist, writer & curator with over 20 years of work within the Oakland, CA/ Bay Area community.

IG: @iamshawnwilliam
Website: www.iamshawnwilliam.com

Made in the USA
Las Vegas, NV
10 December 2022

61707518R00134